KENTUCKY
a photographic journey

D1548651

photography by Linda Doane

FARCOUNTRY
PRESS

Right: Louisville, founded in 1778 by George Rogers Clark and named after King Louis XVI of France, is one of the oldest cities west of the Appalachian Mountains. Today, Louisville is the largest city in the Commonwealth of Kentucky.

Front cover: Churchill Downs in Louisville is the home of the Kentucky Derby. Each year, nearly 175,000 people attend Churchill Downs on the first Saturday in May to watch the "Greatest Two Minutes in Sports." Racing fans come from all over the world to enjoy the pageantry of derby hats and rose garland, mint juleps and wagering, the bugle "Call to Post," and the crowd singing "My Old Kentucky Home."

Title page: Thanks in part to its lush bluegrass pastures, Kentucky is the horse capital of the world. These mares graze at the beautiful, historic Hermitage Farm in Oldham County. Hermitage is a world-class equine operation and sport horse training facility, and has been a working farm for nearly two centuries.

Back cover: Cumberland Gap National Historical Park borders Kentucky, Tennessee, and Virginia. A view from Pinnacle Overlook one early fall morning shows the fog settling in the forest.

ISBN: 978-1-56037-590-6

© 2016 by Farcountry Press
Photography © 2016 by Linda Doane

For more information about our books, write Farcountry Press, P.O. Box 5630, Helena, MT 59604; call (800) 821-3874; or visit www.farcountrypress.com.

Produced in the United States of America.
Printed in China.

20 19 18 17 16   1 2 3 4 5 6

Left: The natural wonder of the sandstone arch at Natural Bridge State Park has stood for millenniums. Formed by weathering, the bridge is 78 feet long and 65 feet high. Some geologists believe that the arch is at least 1 million years old.

Below: Raccoons, like these two youngsters, often den in hollow trees and are known to be highly intelligent. Raccoons are common sights at several Kentucky state parks.

Left: Like many Kentucky bourbon distilleries, the Jim Beam tasting room offers a "treat" of bourbon whiskey at the end of the facility tour.

Right: The Jim Beam American Stillhouse offers guided tours through the entire bourbon-making process, starting with natural limestone water, then mashing, distilling, barreling, aging, and bottling.

Below: Visitors are given access to one of Jim Beam's rackhouses to see some of the more than 600,000 white oak barrels used to age the distillery's Kentucky Straight Bourbon Whiskey.

Above: The U.S. 23 Country Music Highway Museum highlights local country music stars that were born or lived near the highway

Right: Exhibits at the U.S. 23 Country Music Highway Museum include memorabilia from industry stars, like this signed guitar from country music legend Loretta Lynn.

Far right: Country music fans can visit Butcher Hollow, also known as Butcher Holler, the coal-mining community made famous by Loretta Lynn, who paid tribute to her birthplace community in the song "Coal Miner's Daughter."

Facing page: The Old Governor's Mansion in Frankfort, built in 1797, is one of the oldest executive residences in the United States. Known for its rich history, beautiful gardens and interior design, the mansion is open regularly for tours.

Left: Well-crafted white wooden gates and fences border the 34 original structures at Shaker Village of Pleasant Hill. This National Historic Landmark, the largest in Kentucky, is home to the country's largest private collection of original 19th century buildings.

Below: Shaker Village of Pleasant Hill and the Woodford Hounds Fox Hunters join for the annual Blessing of the Hounds.

Above: Jockey silks, or colors, are worn by the jockey to represent a horse's owner. Each owner has his or her own specially designed silk. Over 28,000 sets of silks are registered with The Jockey Club.

Right: A well-worn pair of jockey boots represents the hard work and dedication of these equestrian professionals.

Far right: The U.S. Bank Kentucky Derby Festival Great Balloon Race is one of five events in the U.S. Bank "BalloonFest" held annually in Louisville. On the weekend before the Kentucky Derby, tens of thousands of spectators show up to see the rainbow of colors in these beautiful balloons.

Next pages: Acres of sunflowers line Highway 65 just north of Elizabethtown.

Above: Derby fashion, for both women and men, is planned out many weeks before the big race day. With a nod to European racing events of the past, the Kentucky Derby has become a place to be seen in one's finery.

Left: Hats on display at the Kentucky Derby Museum represent the tradition of the colorful, extravagant headwear associated with the Kentucky Derby.

Far left: Originally a simple chalk circle drawn on the racetrack, The Kentucky Derby Winners Circle at Churchill Downs is now a landscaped area with a red floral horseshoe, reserved for honoring every Kentucky Derby winner.

Above: Lighthouse Landing is nestled on the shores of Kentucky Lake, a mile north of the entrance to the Land Between the Lakes National Recreation Area.

Right: Lake Cumberland is often referred to as "The World Capital of Houseboats." This recreation area is popular with outdoor enthusiasts for boating, swimming, hiking, horseback riding, and world-class fishing tournaments.

Above: Spectators enjoy the view of a favorite Kentucky Derby Festival event Thunder Over Louisville from inside the KFC Yum! Center in Louisville.

Right: The Newport Aquarium allows visitors to safely get up close and personal with sharks.

Far right: The Kentucky Center for the Performing Arts is home to many of Louisville's major arts organizations and offers the finest in music, dance, theater, and more.

Above: Enjoy the quiet early morning training sessions of horses and riders at picturesque Keeneland Race Course in Lexington. Keeneland, a registered National Landmark, is a top Thoroughbred horse racing facility and sales complex. Millions of dollars are spent annually purchasing horses at Keeneland.

Left: November is rodeo time! The Ram Great Lake Circuit Finals Rodeo is held in conjunction with the North American International Livestock Exposition at the Kentucky Fair and Exposition Center in Louisville. Cowboys and cowgirls compete for close to $200,000 in prize money.

Facing page: Rider Joe Meyer and horse Snip compete at the Kentucky Horse Park's largest annual competition, the prestigious Rolex Kentucky Three Day Event. The popular equestrian park features several breeds of horses, educational shows, tours, museums, and world-class equine competitions.

Above: Visitors driving through the Elk & Bison Prairie at Land Between The Lakes get a glimpse of the prairie as it once was. This 700-acre prairie is home to elk, bison, and other Kentucky native wildlife, as well as native plants that were common to the area more than a century ago.

Left: Take a step back in time with the display of Ordovician geology and replicas of ice age mammals at Big Bone Lick State Historic Site in Union, Kentucky.

Facing page: Bad Branch State Nature Preserve in Letcher County is a 2,639-acre preserve with a spectacular 60-foot waterfall. The preserve is owned and managed by the Kentucky State Nature Preserves Commission and The Nature Conservancy.

Above: Learn about coal mining at the Kentucky Coal Museum and Portal 31. The Kentucky Coal Museum is located at a former coal camp in Benham. Tour Portal 31, Kentucky's first coal mine, on an underground "mantrip" shuttle with animatronic miners and an IMAX movie that explains the process of coal mining.

Right: Each year, more than 650,000 visitors tour the world's longest known cave system at Mammoth Cave National Park in south-central Kentucky.

Left: The Switzer Covered Bridge in Frankfort spans the North Fork of Elkhorn Creek and is one of the few remaining "timbered tunnels" in Kentucky.

Below: Rock-climbing enthusiasts come from around the world to climb at Red River Gorge, known for its towering sandstone cliffs, rock shelters, waterfalls, and natural bridges. Red River Gorge, largely located within the Daniel Boone National Forest, is a National Natural Landmark and is listed on the National Register of Historic Places.

Above: St. Mary's Cathedral Basilica of the Assumption in Covington is known for its Gothic architecture and its exquisite stained glass windows, including what is said to be the world's longest handmade church stained glass window at 67 feet tall.

Right: St. Mary's Cathedral Basilica of the Assumption welcomes close to 70,000 visitors each year and is one of 35 minor basilicas in the US. All four major basilicas are in Rome, Italy.

Left and below: Each October, thousands of re-enactors and spectators descend on the Perryville Battlefield State Historic Site southwest of Lexington to pay tribute to the 7,600 casualties from the bloodiest Civil War battle in Kentucky, also known as the Battle of Chaplin Hills. Surging north in the fall of 1862, the Confederate army hoped to claim Kentucky for the South, but Union forces ultimately prevailed. Kentucky remained under Northern control for the rest of the war.

Right: Tally Ho! The Woodford Hounds enjoy the sport of the first formal fox hunt of the year at Shaker Village of Pleasant Hill.

Below: The northern cardinal was designated Kentucky's official state bird in 1926. This handsome cardinal was spotted at the Bernheim Arboretum and Research Forest Education Center, where visitors can watch birds, small mammals, and an active beehive in the center's Wildlife Viewing Room.

Above: Visitors on the winding Skyland Road in Cumberland Gap National Historical Park are rewarded when they arrive at Pinnacle Overlook with spectacular views of Kentucky, Virginia, and Tennessee.

Left: A blanket of heavy morning fog covers Wolf Creek Dam on the Cumberland River in Russell County. One of the largest multi-purpose dams in the nation, the dam generates hydroelectricity, regulates water levels, and forms Lake Cumberland on one side.

Right: This Amish kapp still life is symbolic of their quiet way of life. Kentucky is home to a sizable, and growing, Amish population.

Far right: Ashland, The Henry Clay Estate, is the site of the Great Compromiser's country refuge and plantation. Now a museum and National Historic Landmark, the site features guided tours of the reconstructed 18-room mansion and beautiful grounds.

Below: A beautiful white Gypsy Vanner enjoys grazing at the Aurora Acres Equestrian Center in Crestwood. Aurora Acres specializes in this rare breed, originally bred by gypsy travelers to pull their carriages and carts.

Above: The symbolic birthplace cabin of President Abraham Lincoln recalls the humble single room log cabin where Lincoln was born on his father's Sinking Springs Farm.

Right: The Abraham Lincoln Birthplace National Historic Site in Hodgenville was the first Lincoln Memorial. Built on Lincoln's birthplace site, the marble neoclassical Memorial Building houses the symbolic birthplace cabin.

Next pages: From the Pinnacle Overlook in Cumberland Gap National Historical Park, visitors can watch the sun rise over three states.

Above: The Kentucky Derby Museum adjacent to Churchill Downs showcases the history, traditions, and memorabilia from the Kentucky Derby with interactive exhibits, video presentations, and walking tours of Churchill Downs. One popular highlight is to have your photo taken in the Winners Circle with a manikin of the most recent Derby winner.

Right: Large, colorful, uniquely decorated fiberglass horses can be spotted in several locations around Louisville. This is Gallopalooza–a civic pride initiative that has raised over $1 million, showcased local artists, and beautified the streets of Louisville.

Facing page: The world's biggest baseball bat leans against the Louisville Slugger Museum & Factory building in downtown Louisville. The bat is 120-feet tall and weighs 60,000 pounds. Inside, visitors can see Louisville Slugger® bats being made for today's Major League Baseball® stars. More than 300,000 people visit the Louisville Slugger Museum & Factory every year.
Photo Courtesy of Hillerich & Bradsby Co.

Left: The Old State Capitol, also known as the Old Statehouse, was the third capitol of Kentucky in Frankfort. Built in the Greek Revival style, this building served as the government seat for the Commonwealth of Kentucky for 80 years, and is now a museum and home of the Kentucky Historical Society.

Below: The meticulously landscaped Cave Hill Cemetery and Arboretum in Louisville is known for its exquisite collection of monumental art and for being the final resting place of many prominent citizens. Colonel Harland Sanders, founder of the popular Kentucky Fried Chicken restaurant chain, is buried here.

Above: The Kentucky Vietnam Veterans Memorial is located in Frankfort. Each of the 1,104 Kentucky soldiers that died during the war has his or her name engraved on granite blocks that are part of the base, and the shadow of the sundial pointer touches each veteran's name on the anniversary of his or her death.

Right: The "new" Kentucky State Capitol in Frankfort is the state's fourth since statehood in 1792. Completed in 1910 in the Beaux-Arts style with marble from all over the world, it is considered by many to be one of the most beautiful capitols in the nation.

Above: At the crack of dawn, horses head to the racetrack for their morning training at Churchill Downs in Louisville.

Left: Blazing burners create heat to inflate and make buoyant hot air balloons for U.S. Bank's Great BalloonFest, one of more than 70 Kentucky Derby Festival events that precede the big race.

Far left: More than 50,000 fans annually attend the U.S. Bank Derby Festival Great Balloon Glow held at the Kentucky Fair and Exposition Center in Louisville the night before the Great Balloon Race. Pilots fire their burners just enough to inflate their balloons, but not enough to take off.

IN MEMORY OF
UNKNOWN UNION SOLDIERS
BURIED IN THIS CEMETERY
1861 ◄O► 1865

ERECTED BY
KENTUCKY COMRADES
1914

Above: The Frankfort Cemetery contains the gravesites of many famous Americans, but the most visited gravesite in this scenic cemetery is that of American pioneer and frontiersman Daniel Boone.

Left: From a war that pitted brother against brother, high-ranking Civil War officers, as well as unknown soldiers, rest in peace at Cave Hill National Cemetery in Louisville.

Right: Kentucky State Fairgoers enjoy wild rides at the Thrillway.

Far right: Thousands of visitors annually attend Thunder Over Louisville to view the spectacular firework display that kicks off the Kentucky Derby Festival.

Below: For more than 100 years, fairgoers have attended the Kentucky State Fair for a wide selection of family fun. Largely housed in the 1.2-million-square-foot Kentucky Exposition Center in Louisville, this is America's largest air-conditioned fair.

Above: Wickliffe is considered by many Kentuckians to be the "Birthplace of the Mighty Mississippi" because the confluence with the Ohio River is where the Mississippi River truly becomes mighty.

Left: Louisville is home to the oldest operating Mississippi River-style steamboat, *The Belle of Louisville*. Millions of people have enjoyed traveling inland waterways aboard this historic, century-old paddlewheel vessel.

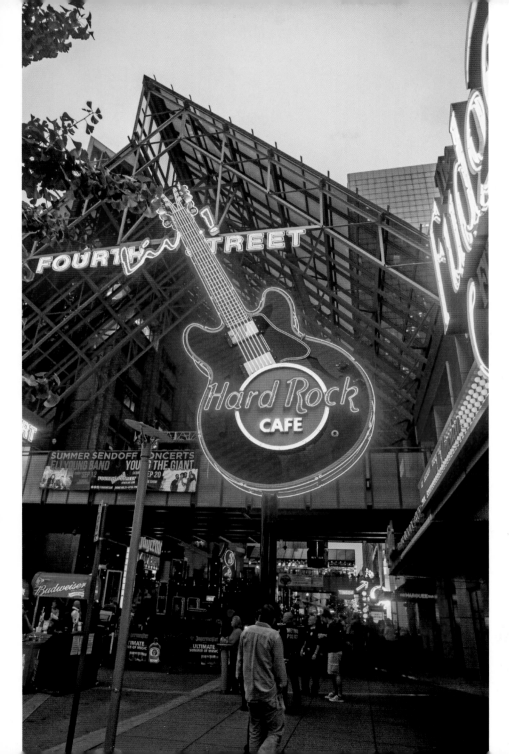

Facing page: Named after the "Big Four Railroad," the Big Four Bridge is a former railroad truss bridge that spans the Ohio River, connecting Louisville, Kentucky and Jeffersonville, Indiana. Today, the bridge has been converted from rail to trail and serves as a popular pedestrian and bicycle bridge.

Left: Fourth Street Live! is a vibrant complex in downtown Louisville known for its retail, entertainment, and restaurant venues, such as the world renowned Hard Rock Café. *Photograph courtesy of Hard Rock Café International (USA), Inc. All rights reserved.*

Below: Through traffic is closed on Fourth Street when evening crowds gather for large special events, such as music concerts, at Fourth Street Live!

Above: Visitors come to the National Corvette Museum to enjoy the many vintage Corvettes in period display, one-of-a-kind prototypes, as well as Chevrolet's newest Corvette on the market. More than 1.6 million Corvettes have been produced at the General Motors plant in Bowling Green, Kentucky.

Left: Colorful, collectable Corvette memorabilia patches celebrate "America's Sports Car."

Far left: The Kentucky Speedway in Sparta is the region's premier motorsports facility, hosting NASCAR, ARCA, Indy Racing, and other exciting events throughout the year.

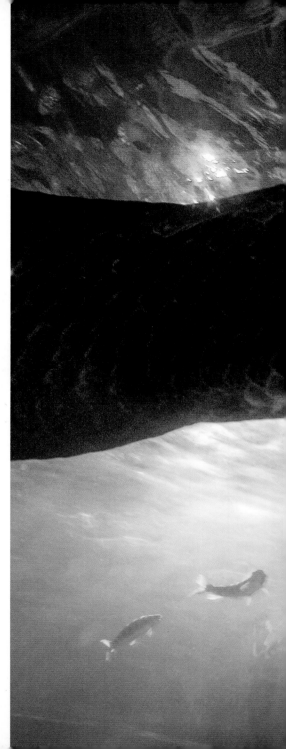

Above: The Louisville Mega Cavern, once a massive limestone mine, is now a multipurpose 100-acre facility beneath the city of Louisville. Sections of the cavern have been developed for tourism and recreation offering tram tours, zipline tours, an underground bike park, rope obstacle course, and a drive through underground holiday lights show.

Right: Climbers at the Louisville Mega Cavern challenge themselves at Mega Quest, the only completely underground aerial ropes challenge in the world.

Far right: Visitors enjoy being "part of the ocean" as they walk through underwater tunnels at the Newport Aquarium on the banks of the Ohio River in downtown Newport.

Above: The colorful northern leopard frog can be found throughout the wetlands, rivers, and streams of Kentucky.

Left: Mammoth Cave National Park, most well known for having the world's longest cave system, also offers beautiful Kentucky hill country and deep moss-covered forests with an abundance of hiking trails, camping, and boating along the Green and Nolin Rivers.

Above: The Kentucky Bourbon Trail Craft Tour® encourages tourists and bourbon enthusiasts to visit seven select craft distilleries throughout Kentucky, sample their spirits, and collect stamps as part of the Passport Program to earn a classic Kentucky julep cup.

Left: Beautiful, detailed life-sized sculptures of Thoroughbred horses by artist Gwen Reardon pay tribute to the Thoroughbred industry throughout Thoroughbred Park in downtown Lexington.

Left: Kentucky remains a top tobacco-producing state. Colorful tobacco plants and iconic black tobacco barns dot much of the rural landscape.

Below: The great horned owl is a common Kentucky resident known for its golden eyes and feathered tufted "horns" that look like cat ears. The tufts are neither horns nor ears, but simply tufts of feathers.

Above: The magnificent fall foliage of the fullmoon maple, also called Japanese maple, is a fan favorite at the Bernheim Arboretum and Research Forest in Clermont. Bourbon tycoon Isaac W. Bernheim gifted the property to the people of Kentucky to become a place where all people, regardless of race, creed, or status, could find peace in nature.

Left: A warm sunset captures a familiar silhouette in Kentucky's famous Bluegrass horse country.

Above: Woodford Reserve is unique in that it's the only distillery to use copper pot stills and a triple distillation process to handcraft its signature bourbon.

Right: The oldest and smallest distillery in Kentucky, Woodford Reserve crafts the Official Bourbon of the Kentucky Derby. Tours of this National Historic Landmark are offered daily.

Above: Farmers' markets can be found in almost every county in Kentucky, offering a colorful mix of fresh vegetables, fruit, flowers, and handcrafted products.

Left: Scenes of rural Kentucky, like this one with old milk cans resting next to a barn, bring a nostalgic feel of days gone by.

Far left: Visitors come to La Grange to enjoy the unique shopping experiences, art galleries, various boutiques, and eclectic eateries. An additional highlight is watching the many trains that roll through the middle of the town each day.

Above: The International Bluegrass Music Museum in Owensboro is the world's only museum dedicated to the international history and preservation of bluegrass music. Learn about the culture, history, and art of bluegrass music, take music lessons, or attend a live jam session or concert.

Right: Old mountain fiddle music was a popular form of entertainment in the isolated Appalachian mountain regions, and was one of the major roots in the development of Bluegrass music.

Far right: The KFC Yum! Center is a large, multi-purpose sports arena in downtown Louisville. The state-of-the-art facility is known for attracting high-profile music entertainment and sporting events, as well as hosting private and corporate functions.

Next pages: Cumberland Falls State Resort Park is named after its spectacular waterfall, the largest south of Niagara Falls. The park is located in Daniel Boone National Forest and offers many recreational activities for the outdoor enthusiast including camping, hiking, biking, fishing, rafting, canoeing, and horseback riding.

LINDA DOANE has worked as a commercial and assignment photographer for 29 years. Her powerful images have won awards at the local and national level as well as featured in many magazines and books. She has assisted in photographic workshops to Alaska, Africa, and Indonesia. Ms. Doane has been a teacher in Wisconsin. She has her master's degree and continues to work as a counselor with people with addictive disorders. Her love for teaching and adventure has lead her to present lectures and photographic media shows to the Sierra Club as well as to many schools, organizations, and associations. Her dedicated work ethic and creative eye has landed her such assignments as: NCAA, Kentucky Derby, political conventions, plus photographing concerts with rock stars such as Cher, Justin Bieber, Justin Timberlake, Pink, Kiss, Eagles, Keith Urban, Jimmy Buffet, and George Strait.

Linda resides in Louisville, Kentucky, loves kayaking, gardening, traveling, horses, and loaded nachos.

Linda is an active member of the American Society of Media Photographers (ASMP) and the Professional Photographers of America (PPA) organizations.

Background image: Quilters and art enthusiasts travel from around the world to visit the National Quilt Museum in Paducah. The museum features rotating and traveling exhibits of exquisite quilt and fiber art, and also offers educational programs taught by master quilters.